Levels Of Love

The definition of love comes in all different forms when asked by different people. Love can be experienced in many ways from different people's individual experience.

Love is a complex and multifaceted emotion that evolves throughout a person's life. While it's difficult to categorize love into specific "levels," as it's highly subjective and individual, I can provide a general overview of how the experience of love may change and develop from birth to the present day.

1. **Infant Love (0-2 Years):** In the earliest stages of life, love primarily comes from the caregiving relationship with parents or caregivers. This love is essential for the infant's physical and emotional development, providing a sense of security, comfort, and trust.

2. **Childhood Love (2-12 Years):** As children grow, their capacity to give and receive love expands beyond their immediate family. They

develop close bonds with siblings, extended family members, friends, and even pets. Love during childhood is often characterized by play, exploration, and simple acts of kindness.

3. **Adolescent Love (13-19 Years):** Adolescence is a time of significant emotional and social development. Teenagers begin to experience romantic and platonic love outside of their family circle. They explore crushes, dating, and deep friendships, often marked by

intense emotions and idealized notions of love.

4. **Young Adult Love (20s-30s):** Young adulthood is a period when individuals explore romantic relationships more seriously. Love during this time may involve greater emotional depth, commitment, and intimacy. People may form long-term partnerships, marry, and start families.

Self-Love: One kind of love talked about in my first book is **self-love**. The love one has for themselves. Knowing the worth of who you are as a person, different from others. This love should have started at birth and continued throughout one's life. This type of love can involve activities like setting boundaries, practicing self-compassion, engaging in hobbies that bring joy, and making choices that contribute to personal growth and contentment. Restructuring this love begins with the desire to want others to love you. The best way to learn love is to find self- love and embrace it.

True Love: The main love you hear people talk the most about is **true love**. What exactly is true love? According to the dictionary it is an unparalleled fondness and devotion for your partner. Seems like there is a lot of true love in the world that leads to divorce. Just saying if true love was the best love, then why aren't people staying together? Why are divorce rates so high? True love can be found but people destroy true love because of environmental factors and differences between the two of them. The experience of "true love" is deeply personal and can vary from person to person. There is no one-size-fits-all answer.

I probably understand the levels of love more than many since I have had to experience them in so many different times in my life. I understand where different kinds of love come from and what it means to different people. When one acts out of hate but really cares for the other person but doesn't know how to show that person how much they really care. I have seen marriages collapse because one of the 2 people is trying so desperately to be noticed and appreciated in a marriage and the other person makes no effort to accept or even recognize them. Many people say they love someone but show that person the opposite. Most of the time the person does this because they don't recognize the other person's feelings even when that person has told them exactly how they feel. The other reason that one may ignore the other person is because they want to feel appreciated and have their own personal desires met. Or sometimes the other person simply just doesn't care. They are only in the relationship because it benefits them in one way or another. Sometimes, people stay together just so they don't have to deal with the embarrassment of going through a divorce when everyone around them thought they were the perfect couple.

In my 1st marriage this was the case. I didn't much care about what people thought about when I decided to get out of my marriage, but I do remember how many people looked at us as the perfect couple. We didn't complain or fight in front of others, and we did show love and affection so why would anyone see anything other than what we showed in public? The most common reason people stay together is for the children. Which never made much sense in my mind. If two people are unhappy together then what energy are they putting on the children?

When I divorced my husband, my children spoke about things we didn't even realize they paid attention to. But for me I didn't want to be unhappy, and I didn't want my children to think what their father and I had was a healthy relationship.

Children learn by watching and they really see more than adults think. It is hard not to show unloving feelings towards your significant other when you know that is truly how you feel.

Relationships in general can be so hard but people focus on marriages the most, because of the long-term commitment one makes when deciding to marry. The funny thing is many people still have friends from grade school that are still a part of their adult life now. Those relationships last just as long if not longer than marriages.

When one seeks marriage, they are seeking a friend for life. They should in fact be their best friend before marriage. Most people don't choose marriage for that reason. Most people consider so many other factors when deciding to get married. They look at finances, statis, social acceptance, physical attraction, religious beliefs, and other things that may be beneficial for wanting to get married. Of course, there is love for one another but before commitment you must decide if it is a healthy love.

Love is a very kind word. It represents a good feeling, and who doesn't want to feel good. Then why might you ask are so many people not feeling this feel-good feeling of love? Love must be perceived as love and often, too many people don't feel loved because they have never felt what love should feel like. The misconception of how love is to feel is always changing in one's mind. An abused child will always see any kind of abuse as love if that is the environment in which love was given to them. When one does show them true love, they will not understand that feeling as love and will even reject it in the beginning. Grandparents may depict love by spoiling the grandchildren with gifts, but gifts aren't love. The gifts are supposed to represent the act of love they have for the grandchildren. But in fact, if a child only receives presents from their grandparents and doesn't spend much time with them, then to them the gifts are love. If someone doesn't give them gifts, then they must not love them anymore. Should that in fact be the case? No but even as adults we look for things to be the place of love. We want to be self-satisfied. But looking back at the definition of love. What is love? Love is a feeling. Getting gifts will make anyone feel good but it isn't love. The gifts are what one does to add to the love that one is given.

There will be many times in your life where you don't understand someone else's love language. Love language is how people express and give love. These love languages represent the different ways people feel most loved and appreciated:

Here is a list of these love languages and different ways people feel most loved and appreciated.

1. **Words of Affirmation:** For individuals with this love language, words are powerful. They feel loved when they receive verbal affirmations, compliments, and words of encouragement. Simple expressions like "I love you" or compliments about their qualities mean a lot to them.

2. **Acts of Service:** People with this love language feel loved when others perform acts of service for them. This could be anything from doing household chores to helping

with tasks. It's about the effort and thoughtfulness behind the actions.

3. **Receiving Gifts:** Some people feel most loved when they receive tangible gifts. It's not necessarily about the material value of the gift but the sentiment and effort put into choosing or making it.

4. **Quality Time:** Quality time means giving someone your undivided attention. Individuals with this love language feel loved when others spend meaningful, one-on-one time with them,

engaging in activities or simply having a heartfelt conversation.

5. **Physical Touch:** Physical touch is a vital expression of love for some people. This could include holding hands, hugs, kisses, or other physical affection. Touch conveys love, comfort, and security for those with this love language.

Let's step aside from that for a moment to think about your current relationships in your life. Are the people in your life showing you love the way they know how to give love? And does that love have meaning in your life? In other words, do you accept the love from others as being love? Some people don't see love and believe everyone has a hidden agenda. Is my co-worker being nice to me so he can show the boss he is a good worker to get the promotion at work? Is my significant other with me because I pay the bills? Do my siblings come around me only because I give them money when they need it? Does my mom not tell me she loves me because deep down she really doesn't?

What are some things you do to show other people that you care about them? Are you affectionate? Do you spend time with them? Are you there when they need a shoulder to cry on? Or do you buy people's affection? Love is such a powerful feeling. When I think of love, I think of giving someone a hug. The physical connection between two people not only lets someone know that you care but lets them feel it as well.

Hugging can be used in many situations and isn't meant as a sexual manner. When someone hugs me, I know it always makes me feel better. Hugging a longtime friend that you haven't seen in a long time. Or maybe a family member. Receiving a hug when you've had a long day and need someone to lean on, or when something unexpected happens and you need a shoulder to cry on. Just think of how you feel when someone embraces you. How does that make you feel? Because in the end we are looking at how love from others makes you feel and how you accept it.

Years ago, on TV there was a group of people just going around filming people while they asked them if they wanted a free hug. Most people said yes and then smiled as they were hugged. This should let you know that physical contact with other people is very important because it provides a connection between people as if they are sharing each other's energy.

Can you think of a time when someone hugged you and you started to feel better? You take a deep breath and sigh afterwards because you almost feel as if the other person took some of the burden from off your shoulders. Maybe it feels like you have a little more strength to get over what you are dealing with in that moment. The reason for this is that energy is transferred at that moment. Now for the believers of Christ. Think about the woman in the bible who knew if she could just touch the hem of Jesus garment that she would be made whole. She touched him and was instantly made whole. Well, if I could go around touching people to get that effect, I would live forever. Lol just saying, that in love, a simple touch can go a long way for someone. If you aren't a touchy person I understand. I used to be so shy that I didn't want anyone near me because I knew I wouldn't be able to hug them back. I simply just didn't know how. I felt awkward about it. When my friends would be going through something I not only didn't hug them, but I struggled with trying to find the right words to console them. It was so hard for me that when one of our friends died when I was just 16, I avoided coming around because I didn't know how to offer condolences. I know that I was probably an extreme case, but over the years I got it. As other people came to my rescue and hugged me, I realized how important it was. So as awkward as it was for me, I started hugging people. Then I liked it because I realized that it not only made the other person feel good, but it made me feel good too because I was sharing love. In the past it just seemed odd because I lived in my mother's shadow, and I was too afraid to come from behind her and her ways just to embrace my own.

Love allows for growth. A simple love for someone can turn into a deep love with time because you are continuing to share each other's energy back and forth. This starts to grow, and the energy becomes more frequent. This is where true love comes in because not only are you sharing a touch but moments of your life with one another. The interaction with conversations and life experiences and time keeps the positive energy alive in any relationship. Once this energy is removed for many factors then the energy becomes weak and sometimes not there at all. This is where people say they have fallen out of love. Some aspect of the energy of love has stopped flowing for whatever reason and there can be so many. From wanting something more or different from the other person, growth and change in your own life, or simply not giving the same energy that you once gave. If you are expecting someone to change because you did, then you may be waiting for a lifetime. Each person changes in their own time and in their own way. It is your job to either accept that person or decide to part ways. Your idea about what you think love is may have changed and the other person may not feel the same. One person always wants the relationship to work and that's why bad relationships drag on for so long because there is never a resolution or a change between both parties to make the relationship stand.

Please don't be one of these people making a relationship harder for the other person because you are stuck in your own ways. You may lose the love of your life because you aren't trying to see how they feel and compromise. When you are in love it is because you shared a good energy but now you are producing a negative one. Take a step back and see why that is. Do you see this happen often in your life? Is it hard for you to maintain a good friendship?

Things to consider.

When you give love is it being accepted?

When you give love, are you feeling loved in return?

Are the actions you are taking making people distant from you and if so, why?

Do you find yourself questioning your actions?

How and when did things in the relationship change?

What factors may have played a part in the change?

Here are a few types of love to be mindful of.

Lustful Love: You cannot love off flesh alone. For if one can only love through a physical connection this is in fact not love but lust. A **lustful love** is mainly used for self-pleasure. If you take the physical component of the relationship away and there isn't anything else left to connect the 2 people, then you know this isn't real love. Real love requires more than physical. Real love is much deeper and should be felt even when there is no physical touch. For real love leaves an energy with the other person and gives them a joyful feeling when just in their presence of that person. Hearing the person's voice or seeing them as they enter the room will bring a smile to the other person's face. There is an unseen bond between 2 people that only they can feel in person or even when far away. The energy is passed back and forth between the two constantly.

If I am being honest. I fell in love with a man that I shouldn't have ever fallen for. I didn't know who he really was and when I found out I was of course heartbroken. I tried to leave this man alone, but his love feels so different from any man I have ever been with. He is so kind and gentle. Even when he doesn't speak, I can feel so much of his positive energy. Why it is this way I don't understand. I just know that this feeling is so amazing that I wouldn't want to let it go ever. When he held me in his arms, I wanted nothing more than to stay in his arms forever, so I don't ever have to have this amazing feeling go away. Love can be so powerful and so addictive because it sends endorphins to the brain feeling pleasure and this strong emotion of love is almost uncontrollable. It makes one feel alive. It can make one feel happy, wanted, and at peace. Love can be so confusing when overthought. But if you look at it for what it is, a feeling, then you can either accept the feeling or dismiss it.

The greatest feeling in the world is love. If you ever get to experience this feeling you always want to feel it. It is a feel-good emotion.

Lack or fear of Love:

There is a phenomenon known as "**philophobia**," which is defined as the fear of falling in love or the fear of emotional attachment. It can manifest in various ways and can be experienced differently by different individuals.

Philophobia might stem from past traumatic experiences, such as heartbreak or betrayal, which can lead to a fear of being hurt emotionally again. It can also develop due to a fear of vulnerability, as love often requires opening oneself up to another person and being emotionally exposed.

Energy levels of love:

Love is not only a feeling but an energy. As long as one generates the energy of love then love will always exist. When one decides to stop sharing the energy of love then the flow of love stops existing. When people are in love you see their energy level change. It is when love is distant that the level of energy is lessened. In relationships the effort to continue to produce this energy affects how the relationship functions. When one of the two parties stops producing the energy of love then the other person loses energy as well. For in a marriage the energy is to become one flow of energy. The energy should continue to bounce back and forth between the two people. Happy marriages strive to keep the energy constant, or some may say they play off one another. Fill in where the other one has weak areas.

The level of love is in fact the energy that love produces. It is important to constantly produce the energy to keep the love strong. If one begins to produce a negative energy, then the love produced will be negative and not received as the love that was once felt. People change throughout their lives and may change the way they love based on their previous experiences of love. It is important that each time one enters a new relationship that they start with a positive flow of the energy of love. If they start a new relationship looking at how they have been loved in the past and that love didn't work out for them then one shouldn't focus on that past love. To ensure a healthy relationship in the future it is important to start off with that feel-good feeling called love. Love someone the way you want to be loved. Learn their love language so they can feel that constant love from you. Give as much time as needed to develop this energy of love because often it takes time for the energy to grow. With that being said, remember to have patience because learning each other's love language takes time as well. It may seem to be easy in the beginning but as time goes on you may forget how to create that same love you did when the relationship started.

In conclusion, understanding and giving love is a profound journey that encompasses a wide spectrum of emotions, actions, and experiences. It's a fundamental aspect of our human existence, enriching our lives in countless ways. It's important to remember that love is not a static feeling; it can evolve and change over time. What might start as a passionate romantic love can mature into a deeper, companionate love in a long-term relationship. Ultimately, the experience of true love is unique to each individual and relationship. It's a feeling that is best understood through introspection and personal reflection.

Here are a few key takeaways.

1. Complexity of Love: Love is a complex and multifaceted emotion that defies simple categorization. It manifests in many forms, from the passionate and intense to the quiet and enduring.

2. Acts of Love: Love is expressed through actions. Acts of kindness, understanding, patience, and empathy are powerful ways to demonstrate love.

3. Communication in Love: Effective communication is key to understanding and giving love. It involves listening with an open heart, sharing one's feelings and needs, and being receptive to feedback.

4. Balance in Love: Finding balance in love is essential. While love can be powerful, it should also allow for individual growth, independence, and self-expression.

5. Love's Evolution: Love evolves over time within relationships. The ability to adapt to these changes is essential for long-term happiness.

6. Continual Learning: Love is a lifelong journey of learning and growth. It involves recognizing that no one is perfect, that relationships require effort and compromise.

7. Energy of love: Love is more than a mere emotion; it's a powerful force that we generate and share. As long as we continue to nurture and generate the energy of love, it will remain a vibrant and enduring presence in our lives. Love is reflected in the positivity, compassion, and warmth we radiate towards others. The energy of love highlights the transformative power of love. It's a continual exchange of energy that impacts not only our own well-being but also the well-being of those we share it with.

Ultimately, understanding and giving love enriches our lives, deepens our connections with others, and brings a profound sense of purpose and fulfillment. It's a journey well worth taking, for it is in love that we find some of life's most profound moments of joy and meaning.

This concludes my series of "The Little Books." I just wanted to say thank you to all that have enjoyed these simple self-help books.

Isha Taha is an author whose passion for writing has been a lifelong journey. Her writing background traces its roots back to her early education, with a solid foundation laid during her academic years at Indiana State University. There, she honed her craft and nurtured her love for storytelling.

With the publication of four books under her belt, Isha Taha has made a significant mark in the literary world. Her debut series, 'The Little Book Series,' showcases her versatility as a writer, delving into various genres, including self-help, suspense, and heartwarming children's tales. Isha's ability to seamlessly transition between these genres reflects her deep appreciation for the diverse facets of the human experience.

Isha's journey as a writer began in her formative years, and this passion for storytelling has only grown stronger with time. Her works not only entertain and captivate but also offer insights that resonate with readers on a personal level. With each page, Isha Taha invites her readers to embark on a literary journey that transcends boundaries and leaves a lasting impact."

www.ingramcontent.com/pod-product-compliance
Lightning Source LLC
Chambersburg PA
CBHW071037080526
44587CB00015B/2657